SUNSHINE COTTAGE SCHOOL
FOR DEAF CHILDREN - LIBRARY
603 E. HILDEBRAND AVE.
SAN ANTONIO, TEXAS 78212-2693

PREEP OF OLD WASHINGTON SQUARE

A Collection of East Texas Tales

by
Sarah Jackson

illustrations by
Delores Jenkins

Halcyon Press Ltd. ★ Houston, Texas

Preep of Old Washington Square, published by:

Halcyon Press Ltd.
2656 South Loop West, Suite 440
Houston, Texas 77054
www.halcyonpress.com

Copyright © 2005 by Sarah Jackson and Delores Jenkins

All rights reserved. No part of this book may be reproduced or transmitted in any form or by any means, electronic or mechanical, including photocopying, recording, or by any information storage and retrieval system, without written permission from the publisher, except for the inclusion of brief quotations in a review.

ISBN 1-931823-25-1 First Edition

Library of Congress Cataloging-in-Publication Data

Jackson, Sarah (Sarah R.)
  Preep of Old Washington Square : a collection of east Texas tales / by Sarah Jackson ; illustrations by Delores Jenkins.-- 1st ed.
     p. cm.
  Summary: A mother cardinal teaches her son Preep about the area where their cardinal family has always lived. ISBN 1-931823-25-1 (hardcover)
  [1. Nacogdoches County (Tex.)--History--Fiction. 2. Cardinals (Birds)--Fiction.] I. Jenkins, Delores, ill. II. Title.
PZ7.J1374Pr 2005
[Fic]--dc22   2005000756

FOREWORD

Some books are based on facts and truth. Others are written simply for the fun of telling a story. Often the best stories try to incorporate a little fact and a little fiction. Historical facts inspired these stories, but as the writing progressed, the author realized she was really writing just for the fun of it and for whatever pleasure it might bring to her own children, Becky and Lois.

Washington Square is a real place, steeped in the history of many centuries. As one of the oldest inhabited areas in the United States, it is still a useful, viable part of Nacogdoches, Texas—a place where birds live happily and in harmony with the other residents there.

Sarah Jackson
Old Washington Square
Nacogdoches, Texas

CONTENTS
Illustrations

1. THE CARDINALS AND THE MOUND BUILDERS 7
   The Mound Builders 6

2. THE MIRACLE AND FATHER MARGIL 15
   The Mission Church 14
   Father Margil at the Creek 18

3. THE RAVEN AND SAM HOUSTON 23
   The Raven and Sam Houston 22

4. THE BATTLE OF NACOGDOCHES 29
   Preep and Billy Jay 28
   The Hammock and Baby Sister 32

5. HOW WASHINGTON SQUARE GOT ITS NAME 37
   The University Building and Uncle Thad 36
   Preep and Mother Cardinal 44

I.
THE CARDINALS AND THE MOUND BUILDERS

"Preep, Preep, PReeeep! Come on in, its getting late, and it's almost your bedtime," Mother Cardinal called from her nest in the big oak tree.

"Oh, Mother," Preep chirped back, "Can't I stay out just a little while longer? Billy Jay and I are racing to see who can get to the ground first."

"No, Preep," Mother called down to him, "Nighttime is almost here, and you know you must be in the nest when it's dark outside."

About that time, a small, dusty-red cardinal swooped in beside Mother Cardinal. Out of breath, Preep asked eagerly, "Mother, did you see that? I was doing the 'spread-wing glide' back to the nest. I've been practicing all day. I can't wait until tomorrow to show my friends that trick!"

"Now, Preep, you don't want to be a bragger. You know to mind your manners around others. Come now, nestle beside me here in the nest," Mother Cardinal urged as she raised her wing, "and I will tell you a bedtime story."

This was Preep's favorite time of day. He loved to hear the stories his mother told him each night.

"Please, Mother, tell me a story of long ago. Tell me a *true* story," he begged.

"Well, let me see," Mother Cardinal began as she scrunched her round, fluffy body into the nest. "Did I ever tell you about the time there were no Cardinals left on Washington Square?" She asked.

"No Cardinals left on Washington Square? That didn't really happen, did it?" Preep asked, his beak drawn down in a frown.

"Oh, the Cardinals did not leave Washington Square because they wanted to. Come snuggle close to me, and I will tell you how it all came about." Mother Cardinal's soft words made Preep feel better. He hopped over close to her and settled down under her raised wing for his story.

Mother Cardinal began, "Long long ago when the world was very new, the Cardinal family first made its home on Washington Square. Of course, it was not called Washington Square at that time—I don't suppose it had a name at all. But that did not matter," she said, turning her head to see Preep's alert little face looking out at her.

"Everything was beautiful. Green trees and flowers covered the land and two streams of clear, sweet water flowed along either side of the village where our family lived. Our friends the squirrels and deer lived here as well as other birds like the Jay family, the Mocker family, and the Sparrow family. Our family was always considered a little bit special, however, because it was the Cardinal who was the adviser to the Indian chief whose tribe lived here. The chief loved Cardinals so much that he took his name from us. He was known as Chief Red Feather," she said nodding happily.

Preep wiggled halfway out from under her wing, "But Mother," he said, "That was a long time ago, and Indians don't even live here now. So what does all that have to do with us?" Preep asked, fidgeting with a feather on his wing. He was wishing he could get away and go play "sky dive" with the other little birds.

"Oh, but it does matter to us," Mother Cardinal answered, settling him down again. "You see, Chief Red Feather was a very special man. If it had not been for him, the other Indians in the tribe might have wiped out our family.

The Indians who lived here then were called Mound Builders. They made great piles of dirt and took squares of mud and rocks and sticks and built big mounds on top of the ground. When a member of the tribe died, Chief Red Feather buried him inside a mound and put some things that he had owned when he was alive in the mound beside him."

"What would they put in with him?" Preep asked, his curiosity returned.

"Oh, things like spears and extra arrowheads, bowls, or beads, and clothes—just all sorts of things—things they felt he might need in Heaven," she explained. Mother Cardinal shifted herself to be more comfortable. "But let me tell you how the Mound Builders nearly wiped out the Cardinal family," she said, getting back to her story.

"One day the little Indian princess, Bluebonnet, the chief's baby daughter, was very very sick. He called the medicine man of the tribe to come and dance a special dance to try to make Princess Bluebonnet well. The old women of the tribe came and rubbed her with oil from nuts and sprinkled rose petals around her bed. All the tribe prayed for her to get well. But she got sicker instead of better. She was hot with fever and so weak that she just lay still with her eyes closed on the pine straw that was her bed.

Chief Red Feather finally decided that she might not get well and that he must prepare a place for her in the mound. With tears flowing down his cheeks, he told the women of the tribe to dress little Bluebonnet in her prettiest clothes and beads. Chief Red Feather placed a bunch of bluebonnet flowers beside his little princess." The tiny red bird shuddered as he thought about Princess Bluebonnet.

Mother Cardinal pulled Preep closer to her as she continued, "About that time, the chief's son, New Moon, came up with an idea that he thought might save his little sister, but it was an idea that would surely ruin the Cardinal family.

This was his plan: New Moon told all the braves in the tribe to take their bows and arrows and shoot every Cardinal on Washington Square. He told them to bring all the birds they killed to the camp by the time the sun set that day. All the young braves agreed that this surely would be a sacrifice for the young princess' life that their gods would like because the Cardinal was the dearest, most respected bird in their tribe. Why, their own beloved chief was named for the Cardinal!

Now in those days when the sun went down at sunset, the sky turned from daylight's light blue into a darker blue and deep purple and then into black night. As the sky began to turn the darker blue, the braves returned one by one with the little cardinals they had shot. They had killed so many birds that they had to bring them in baskets!" She said sadly.

"Just as New Moon had planned, the braves built a fire in the center of the village. All night they sang songs and danced around the fire letting the coals burn low. But all night little Princess Bluebonnet grew sicker and sicker. She did not even try to speak. The women of the tribe sponged her hot forehead with cool water from the nearby stream. As the braves danced and sang, they emptied the baskets of cardinals on the red-hot coals. By this time it was nearing midnight.

Chief Red Feather had never left little Bluebonnet's bedside, and so he did not know what New Moon had planned as a sacrifice for the little dying princess. Just as New Moon tossed the last basket of birds into the fire, Chief Red Feather came outside. When he saw what his son had done, he gave a loud cry of pain as if the killing of the Cardinals killed part of him. Then Chief Red Feather ran to the center of the camp. He cried in a voice so loud that all could hear: 'If the sacrifice of these little birds is not enough and will not please the gods and make my little princess well, then Chief Red Feather will give himself for her life.'

With those words, he threw himself into the flaming campfire. Before New Moon and the others could move to save him, a great puff went up as he knelt down and disappeared into the flames.

New Moon and the other Indians were horrified. They had not expected Chief Red Feather's actions. An odd stillness came over the camp. Not a sound could be heard anywhere. The Cardinals were silent in death. The other birds were crying softly in their nests. The deer and the squirrels hung their heads in sorrow and looked away from the terrible scene. The little princess did not change but lay in what seemed to be a deep sleep. Nothing that had happened seemed to help her get better. Silently the Indians returned to their homes for the rest of the night. Sadness hung heavy over the little village.

But the next morning when the Indians awoke, the sky was red with cardinals flying about everywhere. A miracle had taken place! The beautiful melodies of the birds once again filled the air. And to everyone's surprise, Chief Red Feather stood in the center of the camp with Princess Bluebonnet at his side!"

"What happened?" Preep asked as he looked up at his mother from under her soft wing.

"Red Feather's great sacrifice of love had pleased the gods. They returned the Cardinals to the village and made Princess Bluebonnet well again.

To remind the Indians of this noble sacrifice and to remind them to cherish the cardinals who had paid such a high price for the little princess, the gods made another miracle happen in the sky. Until this day, at sunset the sky turns pink and orange and crimson-red instead of the dark blues and deep purples it had turned before. And Chief Red Feather promised the Cardinals that they would always be safe in this place because he would never allow the braves to hunt and kill them again."

"Oh, Mother, I liked that story!" Preep cried. "Tell me another!"

"Not tonight, little Preep," Mother Cardinal replied with a smile. "Now it is time you were asleep," she whispered, as she fluffed the nest up around Preep and tucked him in for the night.

2.
THE MIRACLE AND FATHER MARGIL

"What—Cheer— Cheer— Cheer! What—Cheer—Cheer— Cheer!" Preep and the two little Jay brothers called from the big oak tree. They were teasing old Mr. Squirrel. Preep watched as the Jays pulled their wings back and dived straight down at Mr. Squirrel, nosing back up into the autumn air just before they touched the ground. Mr. Squirrel paid little attention to them. Busily going about his work, he quickly buried pecans and acorns in the ground. Mr. Squirrel was getting ready for winter. With quick, jerking movements he darted from place to place sniffing the ground until he found just the spot he wanted. Scurrying about, he dug small holes with his sharp claws. His bright eyes flashed as he glanced about always watching for signs of danger.

"What—Cheer—Cheer—Cheer." Preep called out as he swooped down close to the spot where Mr. Squirrel was scratching and digging. He nearly knocked the old fellow over he flew so close.

Suddenly, a familiar chirp floated across the yard. Preep and his friends stopped cold in mid-air.

"Preep, Preep! Just what do you think you're doing!" Mother Cardinal scolded as she flew toward them.

She looked sternly at Preep and then at Billy and Bobby Jay. "I'm ashamed of you three. How could you be so unkind! You know it is disrespectful to treat old Mr. Squirrel in that way. What has he ever done to you?" She asked.

"Oh, Mother, we weren't hurting anything. We were just having fun," Preep replied, looking down to avoid her eyes. "We think it's funny watching him sniff around and then scratch out holes for his silly old pecans and acorns."

"He looks so funny burying everything in the ground," Billy Jay added.

"I believe you may find that you are the silly ones!" Mother Cardinal chided. "Mr. Squirrel hides his acorns and pecans for an important reason. He's storing food for himself and his family to eat later when winter comes when he cannot find food on the trees or shrubs. He's a smart old squirrel. Never make fun of someone who is trying to plan ahead. By storing food for the winter, Mr. Squirrel shows that he is responsible. Grown-ups have to be responsible for their families. When you grow up, you will understand," she said.

The three little birds looked up at Mother Cardinal. Their eyes were wide with interest. She continued, "We birds here on Washington Square are lucky. We have plenty to eat and a nice place to live, but things were not always this way. There was a time when the people, animals, and even the birds on the Square didn't have enough food to eat or water to drink. That's when the birds and animals learned a lot about responsibility, mercy, and miracles."

"When was that, Mrs. Cardinal?" Billy Jay asked. "And what are mercy and miracles?" Asked his brother Bobby.

"Oh, it was a long time ago. Not as long ago as when the Mound Builders lived here, but long ago." Turning toward Bobby, Mother Cardinal continued, "When you show mercy it means you are willing to help someone and be very kind. The miracle came about when Father Margil did something very special."

"Wait a minute, Mother. Please start at the first. Who was Father Margil?" Preep asked.

"Father Margil was a religious man who helped the Tejas Indians who had a village here on Washington Square. The Tejas were peace-loving people. Father Margil was a good man. He taught the Indians how to plant and harvest their crops. He helped them build a mission church, and he was the priest at the mission. The church was just over there," Mother Cardinal added as she pointed with her wing. "Back then the Cardinals could see Father Margil's mission from the big oak tree. His church was one of the first Spanish missions in these parts.

The Indians were happy with their good crops and loved the fine mission. Then almost without warning everything began to go wrong. That year they had so little rain that there were no crops to harvest. The two creeks on either side of the village began to dry up. The land became scorched and cracked. As the corn dried up on its stalks and the beans dried up on the vines, the birds began to fly away from the village to search for food to eat. The Indians became unhappy and hungry. They went to the mission to ask Father Margil for help. The good priest promised that he would pray to God to direct them what to do.

As I said," Mother Cardinal continued, "Most of the birds had left the village to look for food, but a few did not leave. Instead, they flew over to the mission to be with Father Margil, but when they got to the church, they discovered that Father Margil was not there. The birds flew all around the village looking for Father Margil."

"Had Father Margil left too?" Preep asked. His little beak trembled.

"No, Preep," Mother Cardinal replied as she stroked his head to reassure him. "He was walking through the trees to one of the creeks that used to flow beside the village. Finally the birds saw something moving under the trees. They flew down for a closer look. When they saw who it was, they followed the priest to the dry creek bed.

They watched as Father Margil came to a bend in the creek. There he fell to his knees on the dusty ground to pray. He prayed for mercy and a miracle. The birds flew down and perched in a line on a dead limb that had fallen to the ground. Quietly they watched Father Margil. After a long time he stood up. He saw the little birds on the limb and felt their quiet encouragement. Gently shooing the birds aside, he picked up the limb and grasped it with both hands. He drew back and swung the limb hitting a large rock in the creek bed as hard as he could. Nothing happened. He struck the rock a second time, and then a third time. With the third stroke, water poured freely from two holes in the rock.

Both mercy and a miracle had been given. The creek quickly filled with water from the rock so that the Indians and the animals had fresh, clear water to drink. That is the Miracle of Father Margil.

Because of his miracle of bringing back the water, the village was saved," Mother Cardinal said as she ended the story.

The three young birds looked down from the big oak tree at old Mr. Squirrel. He was still rushing around burying his pecans and acorns, but he no longer looked silly to them. They knew they were beginning to understand about responsibility. They knew they were beginning to understand about being grown-up.

3.
THE RAVEN AND SAM HOUSTON

Preep had finished his supper and was resting in the nest waiting for night to come. He liked this time of day. He could look out at the sky and see the beautiful colors at sunset. As he leaned back against the side of the nest he looked up just in time to see a flock of birds flying overhead. He wondered why they were flying so late in the day.

"Mother," he asked, "Where are those birds going? Don't they have a nest to go to like ours here in the oak tree?"

Mother Cardinal smiled at Preep, "Those are special birds, Preep. They are migratory. That means they travel far distances North and South depending on the time of year. When it is cold, they fly away from their homes looking for warmer weather. When it is warm they fly home again."

"I don't think I would like that," Preep said as he fluffed his feathers and nestled his head beside his wing to go to sleep. "I'd get tired flying so far," he added.

"Migratory birds are tough, all right," Mother Cardinal agreed. "They have to be, so they can fly back and forth over such long distances. But one time it was lucky for everyone here on Washington Square that they were tough. It was even lucky for General Sam Houston."

Preep had nearly dozed off when he heard the name Sam Houston. He popped his head up and sang out, "Sam Houston! Wow! How did the migratory birds bring him luck?" (Preep was proud to use the big word.)

"They brought him luck because they had the courage to help General Houston when he really needed help," Mother Cardinal replied.

"You see, Preep, Sam Houston had friends here, but he had a big problem too. He needed troops to fight General Santa Anna and the Mexican Army during the Texas Revolution. Since he wanted to call all the people of our town together, naturally he came here to Washington Square. Men, women, and children came from all over town and gathered here right under our big oak tree. General Houston told them that he needed soldiers for his army, and he asked for men from the town to join him. The general was a good and brave man who wanted Texas to be free from Mexico. He had been going to towns all around Texas to get men to join his army. Many men from our town joined General Houston that day.

But the General's problems did not end there. News traveled slowly in those days. No one knew where the Mexican Army was even at that moment. They could be nearby, or they could still be far away. As it began to grow dark (about this time of day, I guess)," Mother Cardinal said, glancing out of the nest at the deep, pink sky, "a flock of migratory birds flew over Washington Square. They were black birds with large wings. Some say the birds were Crows, and some say they were Grackles, but everyone agrees that there was a Raven with them.

Preep of Old Washington Square

Now when he was young, Sam Houston had lived with a tribe of Indians. He had learned many of the ways of the Indians—especially their love for animals and birds. Because he loved and understood birds so well, the Indians gave him the name, 'The Raven.' After that, Sam Houston always wore a Raven's feather in his hat.

I guess when the Raven was flying over the crowd that day he saw the black feather in the General's hat and knew that it belonged to Sam Houston. Breaking away from the other birds, the Raven swooped down to the ground and landed just in front of General Houston himself. The great general bent down and picked up the beautiful black bird and began to stroke its head.

That's when General Houston saw something hanging out of the bird's beak. 'What's this?' The general was heard to say as he carefully opened the Raven's beak and removed a small piece of cloth. At first Sam Houston didn't know what the cloth meant, but when he looked closer, he knew. The cloth was woven with the colors of green, white, and red—the colors of the Mexican battle flag! And not only that, he found some tiny pieces of seaweed stuck to the cloth."

"What did all that mean"? Preep whispered.

"Well, when General Houston recognized the colors and the seaweed, he knew the enemy had to be to the south near the coast. The bird began to squawk at General Houston in loud, rapid sounds. Some say Sam Houston had learned bird-talk from the Indians and understood the Raven to say exactly where the Mexican Army was holding camp.

Because of the message the Raven had brought, the army of Texans left with General Houston that very night to find the enemy. And I have been told," she added, raising an eyebrow, "that the Raven traveled with the soldiers, flying overhead in the light of the full moon to show them the way."

Mother Cardinal smiled as she finished the story. Her little Preep had fallen fast asleep holding a bit of string in his beak just as the Raven must have carried the bit of flag to Sam Houston that day long ago.

4.
THE BATTLE OF NACOGDOCHES

Preep had decided to go with his two friends, the Jay boys, to old Dr. Jackson's place to look for figs. The little birds were in luck. The figs were plump and juicy—just ripe! Preep loved to eat fruit, and the Jackson's fig tree was heavy with good, fresh figs. Preep and his pals settled down to a splendid breakfast.

Just as he sank his beak into the fattest fig of all, he heard a familiar call: "Preep, Preep—-Where are you, Preep?"

"Uh Oh, that's Mother," Preep thought to himself. As he looked up, sure enough Mother Cardinal flew in and landed on a limb near his. Mother Cardinal loved to eat figs too, and she began to peck at a big juicy one near her limb.

"My, you boys are having a good breakfast this morning, aren't you?" She chirped cheerfully between bites. "Preep, why didn't you tell me these figs were already ripe?"

Before he could answer, she chirped on, "This reminds me of the time your granddaddy got the tummy ache from eating too many figs before they were ripe. Of course, he had not planned to eat green figs. It came about because of necessity."

"'Necessity?" Preep asked, "Who is Necessity?"

"Necessity isn't a who; it's a what." Mother Cardinal replied. "When you do something because you need to, not because you just want to, you do it out of necessity. You see, Granddaddy was hiding from the Mexican Army," she added, knowing it would catch the boys' attention.

"Hiding? Why? And what does that have to do with eating green figs?" The two little Jays asked.

"Haven't your folks ever told you about the big fight on Washington Square between the Mexican Army and the citizens of Nacogdoches?" Mother Cardinal asked.

"No, tell us, please, pleeease," the boys pleaded.

"Well, you see,"... Mother Cardinal began as she took a final peck from a big purple fig and settled down onto the limb beside the boys, "It happened many years ago——long before any of you were born." The three little birds turned their faces upwards toward her to listen.

"It all happened right here on Washington Square. They said the gunfire and the noise were terrible."

"What gunfire, what noise?" Preep chirped excitedly.

"Why, the Battle of Nacogdoches, of course. Didn't I say?" By then the boys were all ears to hear more.

"Granny and Gramp Cardinal (your Granddaddy's mother and father) had their nest in the big oak tree where we live now. One day they looked out of their nest to see soldiers marching up to Washington Square. Some of the soldiers rode horses, some drove wagons, but most of the soldiers walked, carrying guns on their shoulders. They began to set up camp and to build barricades on the Square. Granny and Gramp could see that the soldiers were getting ready for a battle. Since our oak tree is in the heart of Washington Square, Granny's nest was going to be in the middle of the battle.

Your Granny Cardinal was a real fighter herself, but she was no match for flying bullets. She knew she had to get her family away from the nest to a place where they would be safe. But how? Where? All day long she and Gramp worried in their nest as they watched the soldiers below them making their fortress bigger and bigger. How could they get their little family to safety? Where could they go?

Suddenly, Gramp remembered these fig trees where we are now. He told Granny he felt they would be safe and out of the line of shooting if they could only move their family to these trees. Granny and Gramp planned all day how they would move their family to the fig trees. Now your granddaddy and his brothers could fly pretty well even though they were still young, but their baby sister had not learned to fly yet, and this was worrying Granny. How could they get Baby Sister to the fig trees and to safety? It was a necessity to get her to the fig trees—but she could not fly." Mother Cardinal saw the concern in the boys' eyes, so she hurried to continue her story.

Preep of Old Washington Square

"All day long Granny watched from her nest as the soldiers down below stacked bales of hay to make a wall to prepare Washington Square for the big battle that was going to happen the next day. About sunset Gramp had an idea of how to save Baby Sister. Why not take some straw from the bales of hay and weave a little hammock to carry the baby bird! Granny thought Gramp had a great idea.

Darkness began to fall as the soldiers ate their supper. No one noticed the Cardinal family flying down one at a time to pick straws of hay from the big bales. With the help of Granddaddy and his brothers, Granny and Gramp soon had enough straw to weave the little hammock for Baby Sister.

By the time they finished, night had set in, and they were very tired. The only light they would see was from the glow of the coals of the soldiers' campfires below them and from the campfires of the enemy in the far distance. Gramp decided that when daylight came the next morning, they would all move to the fig trees. The night was too dark to fly now. Gramp was so tired, he had hardly snuggled down into the nest before he was fast asleep—sleep he really needed for the day to come."

Mother Cardinal looked straight at her little audience, "Pow! Bang!" she exclaimed to them. "When your Grandfather awoke that next morning, Preep, he heard loud noises that sounded like fireworks on the Fourth of July—-but these sounds were not for fun. He was hearing real gunfire! The battle had begun while his family was still asleep in the nest. Gramp knew they had to act quickly.

One by one he instructed the boys to fly to the fig trees to safety. Your granddaddy went first since he was the oldest and could help the others when they got there. 'Be careful!' Granny chirped as he was taking off. He talked years later about how frightened he had been that day. But he knew it was a necessity, so he gathered his courage and soared off—dodging buckshot all the way.

Finally, all the children had reached the fig trees safely—all, that is, except Baby Sister. Granny said a quick prayer as she and Gramp each took an end of the little straw hammock in their beaks. Baby Sister hopped on, and they began their perilous flight to the fig trees. They were off to a good start, but when buckshot almost hit Granny's wing, she gave a little chirp out of fright. When she cried out, she dropped her end of the little hammock! Gramp tightened his grip on the other end, and Baby Sister bit into the straw with her tiny beak to hold on. Remember, I told you Granny was a fighter. She made a nosedive, circled back, and caught her end of the hammock just as Baby Sister was about to slip off! On they flew, gunfire bursting all around them.

Now what do you think they found when they got safely to the fig trees?" she asked with a smile.

"I don't know," Preep whispered, all big-eyed. Billy and Bobby Jay were too scared to say anything.

"Your granddaddy and his brothers had been sitting in these trees eating green figs the entire time they were waiting on Granny, Gramp, and Baby Sister. And oh, what tummy aches they had! Granddaddy Cardinal never ate another fig after that day!

When the fighting finally stopped, they all flew back home to the big oak tree. You see, Preep, all kinds of things have happened here on Washington Square. But that was the last time we ever had a battle here."

5.
HOW WASHINGTON SQUARE GOT ITS NAME

Preep was busy helping Mother Cardinal clean and dust their nest. Mother Cardinal said that she had put up long enough with the extra twigs and string that Preep always brought into the nest with him. Today Preep's job was to clean things up and to throw away all that he didn't need.

Preep and Mother Cardinal were talking as they worked on the nest. Suddenly, Preep asked: "Mother, why do we live on Washington Square?"

"Why, Preep, don't you like living here?" Mother Cardinal replied with alarm. "Our Cardinal family has always lived in the big oak tree. You wouldn't want to live anywhere else, would you?" Mother Cardinal asked, her eyebrows coming together in a frown.

"Oh, no, I like it here Mother. I didn't mean that. I meant, why do we call where we live 'Washington Square'?"

"Now that's better," Mother Cardinal smiled and sighed. "We call where we live 'Washington Square' for a special reason. I remember my Grandmother telling the story as her mother had told it to her. The Indians never used the name Washington Square. That all came about after Nacogdoches was a part of Texas. Of course, we Cardinals lived here when the Square was only an Indian village," she added proudly.

Years after the Indians were gone, three men who owned this land gave it to our city. Those three men were Hayden Edwards, Charles S. Taylor, and James Arnold. They asked that the land be called 'Washington Square' because everyone thought the name 'Washington' sounded important and special. It reminded them of President George Washington. The men wanted to use the land for a school. That's how we got the Old Nacogdoches University Building too. The town wanted a place where young men could learn their numbers and letters. They also wanted a church on each corner of Washington Square, so the schoolboys would grow up right and learn to do what they should. I don't suppose it rubbed off on all of them though," Mother Cardinal sighed.

Preep looked up at her, "What do you mean, Mother?" He asked.

"Grandma told the story of what trouble some of those school boys could cause. Do you remember us speaking of Great-Uncle Thad Cardinal, or are you too little?" she asked, glancing over at Preep. "Anyway, he learned that school boys don't always stick to their learning—and sometimes they can really cause the mischief!"

"What happened to Uncle Thad, Mother? Did the boys try to shoot him?" Preep asked, imagining the worst thing he could think of.

"Preep! You do let your imagination get away sometimes," Mother Cardinal chuckled. "No, they didn't try to shoot him."

"Well, what did they do to Uncle Thad that was so bad?" Preep asked.

Mother Cardinal put down her little feather-broom and decided to take a rest from cleaning. Because the day was warm, she began to fan herself with the tip of her wing as she began her reply: "To begin with," she said, "you must remember that some people in this world are good and some are bad. Just like some birds are good and others are bad. That's the lesson Uncle Thad learned at the University Building. But Uncle Thad was partly to blame for his troubles because he was a little bit reckless himself." She gave Preep one of those looks that said "You'd better listen to this," before she continued.

"For some reason he did not want to live in the big oak tree with all the other cardinals. He had a good nest here, left to him by his father, but he wanted a new nest in another place." Mother Cardinal gave a little unhappy nod of her head.

"After he and your Auntie looked all around Washington Square, they found just the place where they wanted to build their new nest. The place they found was on the smooth white ledge of a high window at the University Building. From one side of the ledge there was a view of the Square and on the other side there was a view into one of the schoolrooms.

Uncle Thad was very pleased with their choice. He and Auntie were so happy there. They had a secret little 'happy' call: 'Pretty—Pretty—Pretty'. They used the call to show their joy and love for each other. Auntie and Uncle Thad would chirp happily to each other using their secret call: 'Pretty-- Pretty—Pretty.'

Uncle Thad was a curious bird and liked to learn. Each day he could overhear the teacher talking to the class of schoolboys inside. He knew if he listened carefully he could become the most educated Cardinal on Washington Square—but that did not mean he would be the *smartest* Cardinal on Washington Square," Mother Cardinal said tipping her beak high in the air in a knowing fashion.

"You will see what I mean as I tell you more of the story," she said.

"Each day Thad watched through the window pane and listened to the talk inside. Then one day he realized that one of the schoolboys was looking out at him as often as Uncle Thad was looking in! The next day the boy brought cornbread and left it on the window ledge. Uncle Thad and his family loved to eat cornbread. The next day the boy brought more bread. Why, he brought it again and again for two weeks! Uncle Thad became used to the boy and was not afraid of him like he had been at first. He began to trust the boy and would even peck some of the cornbread out of the boy's hand.

One morning while he was eating from the boy's hand, Uncle Thad suddenly felt fingers grip around his whole body. He cried out in fear and pain. He struggled, but it was no use. He was in the tight grasp of the schoolboy's hand—the very hand that he had trusted and had pecked the cornbread from! Suddenly the window slammed shut, and Uncle Thad found himself inside the classroom with all the other boys gathered around. They were excited and loud.

Uncle Thad heard the teacher say, 'Good work, Charles, that bird is just right for our experiments in science class. Bring him here and put him in this box.' Before Uncle Thad could give three tweets he was crammed into a matchbox, and the boy slid the top shut."

"Could he breathe?" Preep asked, out of breath himself.

"Not very well. The boy had made a few holes in the lid of the box—just enough air could come through to keep Uncle Thad alive—and it was dark in there too. Uncle Thad was so cramped he couldn't move a wing."

"What happened to Auntie and their family?" Preep asked tearfully.

His mother looked down at him, "Auntie never had trusted the schoolboy and never ate from his hand. Whenever he brought the food, she and the children always flew from the nest. Uncle Thad was the one who was wild for excitement and new things. But when Auntie saw that Uncle Thad had been snatched away, she flew right up to the window and pecked hard on the pane. She almost broke her beak she pecked so hard, but it did no good. No one noticed her. They were too busy stuffing Uncle Thad into that matchbox."

"Oh, Mother!" Preep cried. "What happened next?"

"That's where the good boys and the bad boys come in, Preep. For every mean person there is usually a good one around somewhere too. But sometimes things don't work out for good right at first.

Uncle Thad felt he had been in the matchbox for weeks, when really it had been only a few days. The box was so stuffy and tight that the time passed ever so slowly for him. The boy, Charles, had caught Uncle Thad on a Friday and so two days passed before the boys were back in class on Monday morning. Uncle Thad had had plenty of time to think about things. For one thing, he was sorry he had ever left the old family nest in the big oak tree. The University Building was pretty to look at, but it was no place for a bird to make his home. He wondered now if he would ever see Auntie and the children again. He hoped they had gotten away and had not been trapped by the boys too.

From inside his little box Uncle Thad could hear the boys in the hallway waiting to come to class. He heard one of them say, 'Maybe today we can begin experimenting on that Cardinal. That should be great fun!' Uncle Thad shuddered as he listened from inside the matchbox.

Suddenly, without any warning, he felt a rush of air. Someone was sliding the top off the box ever so carefully. 'Oh, no, this is the end!' Uncle Thad thought to himself. But to his surprise, he felt gentle fingers clasp his body and heard a kind voice saying, 'Cardinals were never meant for scientific experiments. I won't let them have you.'

With those words the schoolboy who had rescued Uncle Thad ran to the open window and threw him out into the fresh air! Everything happened so quickly that your uncle could hardly catch his breath as he felt himself being hurled into space. He never even saw the boy's face.

Free once again, Uncle Thad gave a loud cry of joy—the loudest chirp he had ever made. He was so happy—he stretched out his wings as far as he could and soared straight up into the sky. He felt he had the strength to fly and touch the clouds! He soared up and then dived straight down flying as fast as he dared. The fresh air, the wind in his face, what joy he felt as he flew around and around Washington Square.

But all at once his happiness changed to sadness as he flew past his nest on the window ledge of the University Building. He was sad because he was thinking of Auntie and the children and wondering if he would ever see them again.

That's when Uncle Thad thought he heard something. 'Could it be?' He strained to hear. The sound was so soft he could not be sure, so he flew closer. 'Pretty—pretty—pretty'—the call became clearer—'Pretty— Pretty—Pretty.' His heart began to pound with excitement. He flew faster and faster toward the call. Then he saw! There in the oak tree in the old nest he had left behind, he found Auntie and the children chirping as loudly as they could—calling him to come home to them."

As Mother Cardinal finished the story, Preep hopped over beside her. "I think I'm beginning to understand, Mother, about living in the oak tree and living on Washington Square," he said. "This is where I belong. It's where our Cardinal family has lived and has been happy all these years. When I grow up I'll build my nest here in the big oak tree too, and I'll tell my children about Chief Red Feather, and Father Margil, and Sam Houston, and Granddaddy Cardinal, and Uncle Thad. But most of all I will tell them about you and how you made me love Washington Square."

Also by Halcyon Press

Barbara Jordan: Breaking the Barriers

by *Ann Fears Crawford*

Ann Fears Crawford's *Barbara Jordan: Breaking the Barriers* is a young readers' biography of this legendary Texas woman, beginning with her childhood in Houston's Fifth Ward. Learn how Barbara Jordan overcame segregated schools and discrimination to earn her law degree and become elected to the state senate and the U.S. Congress. Illustrated. Grades 6-10

ISBN 1-931823-11-1 hardcover 96 pages $19.95

Also by Halcyon Press

Rosa: A German Woman on the Texas Fontier

by *Ann Fears Crawford*

Journey to Texas with Rosa Kleberg as she carves out a new life in a new land. Live the adventure of a German-American woman in frontier Texas. Explore the German colony with Rosa, as she befriends the native Texans, suffers the horrors of the Runaway Scrape, and celebrates Sam Houston's victory over Santa Anna at San Jacinto. She lives to see her family an integral part of Texas's cattle empire—the great King Ranch. Illustrated. Grades 4-8

ISBN 1-931823-09-X hardcover 60 pages $16.95

Halcyon Press Ltd. 2656 South Loop West, Suite 440 Houston, Texas 77054
Call Toll Free 1-866-774-5786 Order online www.halcyonpress.com

Order Form

ISBN / TITLE / AUTHOR	Unit Price	Quantity	Total
1-931823-11-1 / BARBARA JORDAN / Ann Fears Crawford	$19.95	x _____	$_____
1-931823-09-X / ROSA / Ann Fears Crawford	$16.95	x _____	$_____
Order both together (save $6.95)	$29.95	x _____	$_____

Subtotal $_____

Texas residents add 8.25% **Sales Tax** $_____

Total $_____

Shipping is free

WHOLESALERS / DISTRIBUTORS

    Follett Library Resources
    Baker & Taylor Books

Name_____

Ship to_____

Bill to_____

City_____State_____ZIP_____

Telephone_____

Tax ID #_____

Method of Payment:

❏ Payment Enclosed. Check #_____
❏ Please Bill. Purchase Order #_____
❏ Visa/MasterCard/Discover/Amex

Card #_____

Expiration Date _____

Signature X_____